How To Overcome Your Challenges

Master Your Mind, Body and Heart
– Becoming the Iron-Monk

Jean-Pierre De Villiers

WM

How To Overcome Your Challenges

© 2021-2022 Jean-Pierre De Villiers
JPDV International Ltd

First published in the United Kingdom December 2022

ISBN 9798366000741 pbk

jpdv@jeanpierredevilliers.com

www.JeanPierreDeVilliers.com

Contents

Let's Begin. Again

Do you remember being hit by a car? No. I am told I was riding my bike and I was hit by a car. I *know* what happened; I just don't *remember* what happened.

I know we all have things that happen *to* us... *for* us. Most of them do not seem to warrant much thought. Some we can't remember. Some consume our every waking moment. Some we can't forget as much as we'd like to.

Whatever happens, however and whoever it happened; to us, around us, because of or in spite of us, by us... has purpose.

Sometimes it is easy to identify and understand immediately. Other times we are left stunned or bereft of any comprehension or compassion.

Sometimes there is pause for thought – no matter how momentarily – before it evaporates. Other times it has our full and undivided attention. Sometimes lastingly. We hang on to it beyond good judgement or prudence.

Some things make total sense. Some nonsense. And sometimes things are just unfair and make no sense whatsoever.

But that is life. Life is not ideal. Infrequently does reality match our expectations let alone our desires (if we have them.) For most, we embrace the things that match our personnal preferences – our likes and dislikes – regardless of merit; and strive to avoid those that don't.

Sometimes we end up with what we *think* we want. Or end up with more or less of what we want. Sometimes, what was never imagined or desired. Sometimes we don't think. We remain unclear or resist seeking clarity about what real success even looks like – to us – even when given the choice to choose in every or any moment.

What most seek is peace: experienced in the mind, the body and the heart, no matter what shows up. No matter how wonderful or challenging things seem to be.

This book might seem like I am retelling the story of an accident – the story I tell myself about what happened. But it is not about me. It is about your story. The story you tell yourself and the meaning and purpose you give to what happens to you, rather than the cause. The context rather than the content. The message rather than the mess.

It is a story of second chances... or tenth chances. The opportunity to consciously, mindfully and carefully pause and reflect when we are stopped on life's journey.

My book is about how your mind, body and heart overcomes challenges. Any challenge. Size doesn't matter.

There is a theme that runs through every page of this book that will help you do exactly that. Now. Here.

Jean-Pierre De Villiers, Thailand 2022

Beginnings

Do you think your true purpose can change over time or over some significant experiences?

I don't think your true purpose is ever fully developed. Because even if you look at the most enlightened person in the world – let's say Buddha – he never stopped learning, he never stopped growing, he never stopped meditating, there's always a next level.

We are part of nature, and everything in nature is always in movement and momentum.

So maybe your true purpose a few years ago was your true purpose for then, which led you in a certain direction. But now you've been through so much more.

It's possible for you to have a different purpose or a different message. Find purpose in everything you're doing and keep moving forward in more fulfilling ways with a more powerful message.

Keep becoming. Never stop becoming more than you can be.'

◆

MOTIVATIONAL SPEAKER LEFT IN INTENSIVE CARE AFTER BEING HIT BY CAR DURING JOHN O'GROATS TO LAND'S END ATTEMPT

Cycling Weekly

MAN WHO SUFFERED LIFE-CHANGING INJURIES IN HORROR BIKE SMASH WAS RAISING MONEY FOR CHARITY

Devon Live

CYCLIST ON FUNDRAISING MARATHON IS HIT BY CAR

Western Morning News

CYCLIST'S HORRIFIC INJURIES AFTER HIT-AND-RUN NEAR FINISH LINE OF CHARITY BIKE RIDE

Yahoo News

◆

I have a different energy now. Since my accident, I mean. I've become a different person.

For some people and their friends and family, that might be troubling. But I'm not troubled by it all.

In fact, I celebrate it.

Someone told me not so long ago, 'Don't worry JP, you'll get back to who you were before.' My response was immediate and emphatic: 'I don't want to go back to who I was before.' That's not a slight against the old me. I'm proud of everything I've achieved – often in spite of some real obstacles and difficulties – but we can't and shouldn't stay the same people forever. Sometimes something happens that transforms you for the better.

Being who I was for so many years served me so well. But as I've been saying time and again to clients and rooms full of people for many years: 'If you're not going to keep growing, you're going to start dying.'

Intensity

One thing that I was definitely ready to let go of was my intensity.

I know I'm quite an intense person anyway, and plenty of people have suggested that to me throughout my life, so it wasn't a shock revelation. I still have that character trait, and that's always going to be who I am. But having the constant need for intensity in my life, this drive to go fast at all times and at all costs, can get almost addictive. It went into absolutely everything that I did and really became one of my main defining features as a person. I was fast, quick, intense, loud. It was kind of taking over and becoming the main reason for doing what I did.

Around two or three years ago though, a nagging thought started to creep in that I was feeling a bit burned out. Like there's only so much steam available, and I was beginning to run out of it. This intensity had pushed me to achieve so many amazing things that I was – am – truly proud of, not least in my speaking, coaching and personal training careers, but it was also sometimes a burden that was sucking energy out of me.

Throughout my life, I've found that it takes me around three to five years to attain notable success that's recognised by others. Once I've been in an industry or field for that length of time, I'll have become one of the people that others are talking about – someone at the top or near the best of their chosen profession. I don't say that to brag, just to explain how the intensity works and how, after so much hard work and full-on determination for a lengthy period of time, it's perhaps no real surprise to find that reaching the peak coincides with a slight sensation of overdoing it. I'll have been all-in during those years. I'll have learned what needs to be done, and through my experience, I'll know the process I need to go through to reach the top. I'll put the work in and make it.

I never doubt that.

But operating at such a breakneck pace eventually has to take its toll. And it doesn't just affect you as an individual; it spreads into every aspect of your life, not least your relationships and your business career. To some people, especially those closest to me, this effect was probably obvious as it diminished my ability to always be the best person. Yet other people would have likely had no idea that the intensity was consuming me in this way. From the outside, they'd have seen a person who had it all sorted out and under control. As if their mind, body and life were always in perfect shape.

There's a great saying, though: *Don't compare your insides with other people's outsides.*

I think that's a beautiful shorthand for noting that you never know what's going on behind the façade a person presents, and equally, you have no idea what sort of front you present to others. You might be surprised how people see you and shocked to learn what's going on in someone else's life.

Anyway, I'm always the first to put my hand up and say I haven't nailed life. And to be honest, it's a fair bet that anyone who tells you they have is either hiding something from you or from themselves. People in my coaching community know I'm never preaching that I'm perfect or that I've cracked the game of life.

Despite being a peak performance coach, I'm also honest enough to say that I haven't reached my own peak yet.

Scaling peaks requires constant climbing, upward momentum, looking up at your own personal summit and striving to reach it. To some extent, the top of the mountain should always be tantalisingly just out of reach – as you round each bend, you find a little bit more climbing to do – so that you always move forward and never become complacent.

I invite every single one of you reading this book to climb together with me. There will be times when we stumble and fall down a little. That's OK. It's not always going to be a straightforward journey, and we'll need the resilience to prepare for that and be comfortable with our slips. We'll dust each other off and continue, and we'll celebrate each and every one of our individual and collective accomplishments along the way.

So this intensity that was starting to have a negative effect on me, I didn't know how I was going to let it go. And it wasn't always a conscious thought in my mind either. I wasn't overtly or clearly thinking, 'Hmmm, this intensity may be problematic, how can I free myself from it?', because it was a part of who I've always been. It was part of normality for me.

Ever since I was a young child, it's been part of my DNA.

◆

Can you take us back to your childhood and how that got you to where you are today?

My mom did the best she knew when bringing us up. I have two younger siblings, Andre and Sean. We live all over the world, and we're all self-employed and entrepreneurs; I think largely because of what we experienced growing up we all chose to create our lives. And one of the things we witnessed growing up was a lot of suffering. I watched my mother her whole life be in jobs she didn't love, just for one reason: so she could feed us and take care of us boys. It was up and down. Sometimes you had no money, sometimes you did. Sometimes you had little bits, and then there was nothing.

When I was ten years old, my mom sat us down and said, 'You're going to have to live with someone else because mommy can't afford to look after you anymore.'

Andre was eight, and my little brother, Sean, was four years old. Can you imagine?

My mom hardly owned anything. She had an old car for a while that didn't work most of the time if I remember correctly, and it stood outside our little apartment. The only thing my mother really owned was her kids. She is so strong. You've got to be really strong to face up to the fact that you can't afford to keep your kids anymore.

What went through that ten-year-old's mind?

It was what I knew. I grew up in Namibia and South Africa. I witnessed a lot of things going on around me, and I could never really trust what my dad was going to do next. So I was always in fight or flight. Always in survival mode. My mom has a sister, my aunt, who lived a few miles away, and at that point, they were bringing food and shopping to us at our house. I was wearing clothes passed down from my cousin Marc. I was wearing his clothes, Andre was wearing my clothes, and Sean was wearing Andre's clothes. So it was already our life.

I'm not religious, but I believe in setting intentions, having faith and gratitude. My mom just kept saying: 'Please, God send me a tall, dark and handsome man. Please, God, send me a tall, dark and handsome man.' And my stepfather, then to-be stepfather for quite a few years, was tall, dark and handsome. He's not perfect, but who is? He took us out of that situation. Even though he had kids, he took my mom and her three children, and we went to live with him. And that was a real change.

It was difficult then because we moved to a better area, but we still had the same amount of money really. So now I was getting picked on because I didn't have the same haircut as the other cool kids, I didn't have the right shoes because all the kids had Nike, Adidas, Reebok and so on. From that year when we moved, I just got bullied for the rest of school. I went to a few different schools. I once asked my mom if I could change schools, and I told her it was because I wanted to study another subject, but I just couldn't handle the bullying anymore.

And at that point, did you feel like a victim?

I felt not only sorry for myself, but I felt angry with everyone else that wasn't experiencing what I was experiencing. I would actually hate the popular kids. You don't know what you don't know.

But looking back, there were a lot of things missing. So I just saw what was missing and I saw what was wrong. And at ten years old, I made a decision: 'You know what, I'm not going to be a victim of this. I'm going to go out and create'. And I started creating, and I went to work. I started working at the age of ten.

It gave me a real hunger. I started washing cars at ten, delivering papers on a paper round the following year. I washed windows at a petrol station. At twelve, I started taking people's trolleys to their cars outside a shopping centre, and I would stand at the door and say, 'Can I push your trolley to your car?' Some of the time, people would give me a tip. I was twelve, and I was cute.

I began to make my own money. And at thirteen years old, even though I was too young, I got a job in a fruit and vegetable market. All I did was stack shelves and stand at the till from thirteen to eighteen years old on weekends, evenings and school holidays, packing people's bags.

I actually did really well from that, but I didn't go on holiday much.

I did, however, buy my first pair of Nikes at thirteen. I'll never forget those black and white Nikes in the orange cardboard box, and I'll never forget the leather smell, even though I'm vegan now. Because when I was nine, ten, eleven years old, I would take my friends' old shoes when they got new shoes. I'd say, 'Can I have your shoes?', and I would polish them up nicely. We have this white cleaning liquid in South Africa called Handy Andy. And I would put them in a box, and I would wear them for a while until they were really knackered.

I just started hustling and working from a very early age, but I think because I was so angry and sad, I did it at such a speed that I ended up doing it for all of my adult life.

◆

Accident

It may not always have been straightforward or easy, but I know I didn't have the worst life.

I'm well aware that there are plenty of people significantly worse off than I was, so despite all the difficulties our family endured, I choose to focus on the ways in which I was privileged and lucky.

Well, I do now at least.

As I was growing up, I wasn't always so sanguine. Whether it was from the trauma of my father's suicide, the bullying at school, the lack of money, the absence of certainty and safety or more likely, a combination of all those factors, I spent much of my youth chasing things for reasons I couldn't explain. And to be frank, I did pretty damn well out of it in the end.

I got into personal training and found out that I was good at motivating and inspiring people. I won awards and started motivating and inspiring people in other ways, getting into public speaking and coaching, working with celebrities and some of the world's most successful business people.

I've now published nine books, and I operate in a dozen countries where I can regularly share my knowledge and experience with incredible people and get to do what I know and love.

I'm blessed.

But then came the accident, and in less than one, very abrupt second, my life and my perspective were flipped on their head.

As I lay on my hospital bed in June 2019 – the accident had happened the month before, but it took me a number of weeks to fully wake up and regain any sense of thought beyond my current situation – something else just as powerful struck me. I thought, 'Huh, how funny. All of that chasing after things got me wedged between a tree and a metal barrier on the side of a road. I don't remember the accident at all.'

I have no recollection of the incident itself, but I know I was travelling downhill so was presumably going at a fair speed with my head down and my eyes locked on the road directly in front of me. There's no way I'd have seen the car coming from a distance until it was right there, striking my front wheel head-on, after which it just carried on driving without a pause.

Like it had only been over a tiny pothole in the road.

The reason for this thought being so much more important than merely a passing, throwaway note in my mind is that I realised if I couldn't remember any aspect of the accident, then I was extremely grateful – and bloody lucky – to have woken up from the experience at all. It's a deeply strange insight to have stared death in the face without even appreciating that had happened, and then to be aware that had I died, I wouldn't have known anything about it. I simply wouldn't have woken up, and that would have been it.

Game over.

I'm not saying it's a better or worse way to go than any other, but I can't quite convey what an odd, sobering sensation it is to know that I came so close to having the lights turned off permanently without any knowledge it was about to happen. I would have just been merrily cycling down the road, and then bang, I wouldn't have existed anymore. Does that make sense? It's a very close-up study of your own mortality – something that, day-to-day, we tend to give little consideration to.

It occurred to me in that moment, if I had passed away right there on that roadside without any idea of what was coming, what regrets would I have had?

◆

At that moment, when you woke up after the accident, having that realisation of your injuries and what you'd been through, was there any point when you wished your life had been taken?

I just didn't. I think maybe I would wake up at times and have a little cry or something, but I just didn't really ever feel that way. Strangely enough, while still in the Intensive

Care Unit, I would say things like, 'I've got four months, I'm going to do an Ironman triathlon in September'. And everyone would look shocked and say, 'What? You're delusional'. But that would just galvanise me even further: 'You don't know me. You don't know me. I'll show you'.

And then I got to August and realised, 'You idiot! What were you thinking?!'

But I was visualising myself on my bike.

And I always tell this as a joke: I was lying in hospital with metal through my legs, weights attached to me, locked down on the bed and bandaged up. I had a black eye, and I remember waking up, looking at my body, remembering where I was and saying: 'This is so good for marketing!' As a speaker, you need to have a powerful story. And I just couldn't help myself. It made me laugh.

My story was now super-awesome!

Only two weeks after leaving the hospital, one of my heroes, David Goggins, a guy that made me start running ultra-marathons, was coming to London. So I said to my family that I've got to get to London. And I found a way to go to London by getting driven there.

I had a wheelchair in the hotel, and I was able to get the time from my friend Nick James, who ran an event called 'Expert Empires', and he let me in just before David Goggins was talking. I managed to stay till the end and then left, lay down in the car, took my pills and went home. Oh, and because I showed up, Nick and his team got me a one-to-one sit down chat with David Goggins. I'll never forget that!

I'm always forward-thinking. So no, never. I never once thought that I wish I had died.

But I believe that God and the Universe really gifted me that crash and that they said, 'I'm going to give you this experience that's going to change your whole life, but you're not going to feel it,' because I don't remember the accident. At all!

I choose to believe that my memory being blacked out is a gift from God. Because imagine what a different experience it would've been if I remembered that; if I was fully conscious.'

♦

Regrets

It felt like I needed to remember my own advice.

Advice that I'd been handing out to thousands of people over the years and which is printed in one of my previous books: *Live without regrets. Own your life.*

If that's the case, why was I lying in bed thinking about my regrets? As I explained earlier, I never said that I'd *nailed* life.

I'm proud of the fact that I am and always will be a work-in-progress and that I haven't necessarily figured every single thing out yet. But I promise, I'll constantly keep striving towards that goal, and I hope you will too.

However, in that moment, I realised there was one respect in which I needed to do a better job of practising what I'd preached. I thought, 'Right now, if I had passed away and been able to look back on my life, would there have been any regrets?'

And I knew there was one: I wasn't dedicating myself 100% to the things I was passionate about.

I was definitely doing some things – even many things – that I felt passionate about, but not everything. Not 100% of the time.

As I'm sure you'll agree, it's easy to get caught up in other things. In this life, we seem duty-bound to stay busy, busy, busy, and that's what I was doing. Forever flat-out busy but not always totally committed to my true cause. It was an excuse – an evasion.

You may know this feeling too.

Sometimes, that even means you're doing stuff that you really love, but it's not necessarily directed at your chosen end goal in any purposeful way. It might be nice, but what's its value to you and the world? I knew something had to change. And it was all linked to that innate intensity of mine too.

That was a big wake-up call for me. I knew I was selling myself short unless I slowed the heck down. It was a big lesson to me, and I don't believe I would ever have learned it unless I'd had that accident and spent days, weeks and months laying in a hospital bed. Strange though it may seem given what I had to go through, the crash was a blessing.

So when I finally got out of hospital, I went to work.

Positivity

◆

CHARITY CYCLIST ON LONG ROAD TO RECOVERY AFTER FACING DEATH IN NORTH DEVON HORROR SMASH

Devon Live

CYCLIST WHO WAS 'NEARLY KILLED' IN A HIT-AND-RUN WALKS AGAIN ONE WEEK AFTER LEAVING INTENSIVE CARE

Daily Mail

◆

I truly believe that I've found my gifts in life. I have more than one gift, as you do too, but I'm certain that I've discovered those available to me and have maximised and amplified them to the best of my ability.

As well as that, since my twenties, I've developed

a strong mindset that has stood me in good stead for challenging times such as these. That mindset means that I've been able to stay extremely positive. Not foolish, naïve or ignorant, but positive, resilient and confident.

These are potent traits that we can all nurture for our lifelong benefit.

Thanks to my positive mindset, I've never considered myself a victim at any point during this life-changing event. That's as true as I write today as it was when I first sleepily parted my eyelids, saw I was surrounded by and attached to myriad machines and hospital equipment and heard people say, 'JP, you've been in an accident.' I haven't once caught myself thinking, 'Woe is me.'

Now some people might say, 'Ah, JP, well it's alright for you. You were obviously born with that outlook on life.' But that's categorically untrue.

It wasn't until a certain point in my twenties that I realised I had to make a change to my mental approach. Before that, I'd spent practically every day thinking, 'Woe is me.'

I wasn't in control of my life; my life was in control of me. Like being on a rollercoaster that takes you round and round and up and down, I didn't think I could choose my direction. Instead, it was perpetually chosen for me. And it felt as if I was just trying to get through life, rather than striving to reach the peaks I was capable of.

Do you know how that feels? Can you relate to that out-of-control sensation?

Well, I'm here to tell you that you too can change your mindset and become more positive, just like I did. It'll take time, and you'll need to be consistent with your practice. Sometimes you'll fall or feel like perhaps nothing's changing, but if you bounce back up and stick at it, one day you'll be in a situation and you'll appreciate that you're facing it with the mind of a positive and resilient person, not someone who feels like they've had another unlucky break. It makes a massive difference to the way you experience life.

In the recovery from my accident, I made full use of my mindset to go to work on my body.

Recovery

I would say that the skills I've been practising for the longest time and banging on about in public and on social media for the longest have been mental and physical mastery.

They've been the things I talk about the most and what I've become best known for; my USP if you like. Whether you call it self-mastery, personal development, peak performance, life coaching, self-reinvention or whatever else, I've been cultivating and sharing my knowledge about it for a long time. But rather than helping other people overcome their own obstacles, now I was using my expertise explicitly to take care of myself.

That's why this accident was the greatest thing that had ever happened to me. Because for all the years that I've been speaking professionally, everything that I've been speaking about and delivering with so much passion, enthusiasm and energy to audiences around the world are skills that I've been practising in my own life.

And now, here I am, with the things that are keeping me mentally and physically afloat, getting me back to full capacity and literally saving my life, being the same skills that I've been developing and teaching for years. It's more than a simple coincidence; it's a validation of everything that I've practised.

Whether it's getting my movement back, regaining focus and mental strength or creating a positive and powerful message, they're all reliant on the mindset that I've cultivated and talked about again and again on the stage, on social media, with my online coaching community and with my private executive coaching clients.

So, with effort, these same tools can be available to you too.

God forbid you're ever involved in a serious traffic accident, but life throws all sorts of different challenges at us, and the key is knowing that we're equipped to respond in a useful way. Not cowering in some corner, afraid of what's come our way, or giving up because it's too hard or too dark to deal with but confronting it with the skills we've developed.

Even if you feel like those skills aren't relevant to your life right now, you can be absolutely sure that you'll need them at some point in the future. And when you reach that stage, it's too late to say, 'Hang on a moment world, I just need to spend time mastering my mind and body. I'll see you when I'm ready.' The earlier you start practising, the better. (Equally, of course, it's never too late to start. Don't get depressed believing you've missed your chance – think about it, would it be preferable to begin the process of strengthening your own mindset now or tomorrow? Why would you waste another day?)

Sometimes when I speak, it's clear that some people just aren't getting it. For example, I often repeat the message *Fitness is not about fitness* when I'm talking at an event. That regularly receives a few confused frowns from amongst the faces in front of me.

What I mean in that instance is that *fitness is about more than simply getting fit.* It's about who you become in the process.

Do you see how that connects to what I'm discussing here?

Practising something is about the process. A goal isn't only a goal; it's also about how you change for the better while you're trying to attain it.

So I've been practising, teaching and learning this stuff over so many years that when the time came, I had this toolbox full of helpful gear ready to go.

After I had the accident and came out of hospital – even when I was just starting to become properly conscious after a couple of weeks in the ICU – I was able to just reach into the metaphorical toolbox that I carry with me everywhere. 'I know what to do here,' I was able to tell myself.

If I was feeling a bit low, for example, I could deal with it without moping around or getting stuck into some awful spiral of depression. It's all simple stuff once you have access to it, but the trick is to prepare in advance so that it's nearby when you need it the most.

I've said enough about that process in the past. I've got other books and posts and talks that cover it. What I really want to share with you here is about how you can change your future. I know because I've done it.

I know, because at some point in my life, it occurred to me that if I could lead myself in the wrong direction, as I had been doing, then surely I could start to lead myself in the right direction too.

◆

You mentioned that when you're going through the dark moments, you have a toolbox to tap into. So what's the best tool that you have to hand for that?

Gratitude.

That's the first thing. 'I'm not dead!' So really, I don't have anything to complain about. I still have another chance at life.

Taking responsibility and being grateful: I'm still here. I'm not going to blame anyone because just by blaming someone, I give away my personal power and I already start to feel bad. Before anything else happens if I just blame someone for anything – at work or about an accident – I now feel bad.

You can't blame someone and feel fantastic about it.

I made sure that I kept the right people close to me. And I'm very blessed. I am incredibly grateful for all the people in my life and all the support I receive. Also, honestly, I couldn't have done this without my partner. I really couldn't have!

I'm just so grateful that she was there. In the Intensive Care Unit for two weeks, she sat there from 10am until night-time with me in a drug-induced sleep next to her most of the time. All I would do was wake up for moments and then go back to sleep for the rest of the day. I was very fortunate to have her by my side, supporting me.

◆

Rock Bottom

At what age did you realise your true purpose in life?

The reason I got into personal development and self-enrichment and helping others be better is that when I was twenty-three years old, I was a full-time DJ, and I ended up doing a set in Riga, Latvia. Despite this enormous opportunity for me, the next morning, hungover, intoxicated and depressed, I had reached rock bottom.

I realised that I moved from South Africa to the UK on my own as an adult. And how can I become so self-destructive on my own and blame someone else? I thought, 'If I can do this on my own, and go in the wrong direction, I must be able to figure out how to go in the right direction.' I just got to figure out how.

So I did it just for me; I had no intention of helping anyone but myself – at first.

But after two and a half years, it was like a ripple spreading outwards. The more impactful the ripple, the further the effect goes.

First of all, I changed, then my work changed, my friends changed, people around me started to change. And they began to say things like, 'Man, this is really amazing what you know, what you're teaching and look how much you've changed.'

And at that moment, being twenty-five years old, I realised that, *yes, there are no guarantees in life*, but maybe, just maybe, if my father had the environment, the support, the knowledge, the awareness that I had now gained through my self-education, maybe he would still be around.

That's when I knew. I knew I wanted to take what I knew, keep learning and share what I know with people who wanted to listen or needed to hear it.

I will dedicate my life to helping people transform their lives by me doing it first, walking my talk, practising what I preach – which has been my tune all my life – and then sharing it with others.

◆

If you know my story, then you'll know that the rock-bottom moment in my life came in Latvia.

I was a DJ, and this set, playing at midnight in front of thousands of ecstatic fans, should have been the high point of my career. Instead, afterwards, I found myself getting drunk alone in a strange city experiencing a long, dark knight of the soul. I needed help – or more accurately, I needed to help myself. I realised that I had brought myself to this position, so I reasoned that I should equally be able to get out of it, too.

I wouldn't have been the first person to have the thought that something needed to change.

The notion is common enough, but how often do we fail to act on it?

Perhaps you've had an idea of reinvention or transformation. Perhaps, 'I want to get healthier, I want to earn more money, I want to have more high-paying clients, I want to leave my job,' sounds like a familiar train of thought to you?

But then, in the next breath, maybe you're feeling powerless to do anything about it and quickly discard the idea before moving on to whatever catches your attention next.

The reason for this is because the idea remains just an idea. Nothing happens. It's a thought alone with no plan of action. Whereas if you're going to master anything in life, you have to get to the next level of mastery: practice.

Trust me; I don't think I'm different from or better than anyone else. I'm not saying it to be condescending. In fact, I'd even go so far as to say that I probably started the first twenty-plus years of my life in a more negative mental space than most.

I always considered myself to be one of society's biggest victims. I couldn't see anything good happening in my life, either then or in the future. But gradually, I started to have more ideas and envision glimpses of a better outlook.

There are all these little touch-points in my life – whether it's from working out, hitting rock bottom in a flash hotel in Riga, having a role model or mentor or being influenced in any other way – that led to me starting to question,

'OK, what do I need to do to take this idea and make it part of my DNA?'

I had to find a way not just to have the idea, but to practice this new thing that wasn't previously part of who I was, and to keep practising it so that one day, it became my nature.

The simple principle applies to any transformative thought you might be having:

Idea > Practice > Nature

Responsibility

◆

Your father died by suicide when you were thirteen. How did that affect you?

Imagine there's no financial wellbeing or safety.

You're not popular – you're actually quite the opposite; you're just an easy target for everyone.

At this stage at thirteen, I've probably been to about six different schools, because we moved around so much. But you're a kid, and the only real positive thing you feel you do have is your parents if you're lucky enough. And I had my parents even though my father was hardly around, but every time I would see him, and he'd come to visit, I'd be like, 'Yay, daddy!'. He was still my hero.

So now one of the things that I was given at birth, and that was always mine, and that I loved was gone. I felt like, how can I be good enough to be here, if my own father doesn't even want to hang around for me?

Do you know why he ended his life?

Never ever judge a bully. Never ever judge someone that's going through something, because no-one comes into this world emotionally unravelled, not one single person. But I didn't know this before, so I was angry with my father for a long time.

And just recently my mother shared something with me that I didn't know before. You see, I already knew that my father was into loads of bad habits such as gambling and cheating and not being around and all the bad things you can say about a father or a mother. All of those things, my dad was that - physically abusive, emotionally abusive. But what I didn't know is that when he was five years old, living in South Africa, his mother got remarried, and she had a new son, his then half-brother.

So my dad and his real brother were born in South Africa, and his mother remarried an Englishman, and she wanted to move to the UK and couldn't take my father or his brother with her. She left anyway. She left her own children in an orphanage.

I didn't need to hear more because how can you ever feel in your life that you are enough if your own mother leaves you behind for a better life?

So he never felt *enough*, ever.

Which is why he took immense risks and gambled and cheated looking for significance and was always after the thrill and the rush, and he just became a troubled man.

Does that change the meaning that you gave your father's death?

Yeah, as I said, I've been going to work on myself most of my adult life, so in my early twenties I started to see a coach to deal with my *father issues*.

And I learnt to forgive.

That was the most powerful thing. Forgiving others is not just for them; it's also for you. When I started to forgive my father when I was about twenty-six or twenty-seven, it really freed me up, and I forgave him. I honestly forgave him with all of my heart.

But when I found out more about his life, it's like I went from forgiveness to feeling sorry for him. And I remember exactly where I was, looking up and just saying, 'Dad, wherever you are, I promise you that your life was not in vain. My life will be your greatest success.'

◆

So would you agree that if there's something in your life that you want to master, that if you've had an idea about an area of your life that you want to improve, that if you're sufficiently dedicated to practice it for long enough, eventually it will become your nature?

That's what it takes.

It doesn't sound like a particularly complex or demanding process when it's put like that, but for many people, it feels like an impossible burden. Because that one small process seems to ask so much of us: we must be willing to re-organise our lives and make time and mental space when there would appear to be none. We have to make a long-term commitment and prepare for upheaval to an established routine. However, if we're true to ourselves, we know these are excuses which we must cut out.

In our lives, if there's something we want to do badly enough, we make time for it somehow. We prioritise it over some other part of our daily schedule.

So the questions you have to ask yourself are: *How much do I want this change? Do I want it so much that I'm prepared to put it first and make it my priority?*

It's up to you – no one else – to take responsibility for everything that is and everything that isn't in your life. Only once you've accepted and taken that responsibility are you ready to fully dedicate yourself to the practice needed to turn a transformational idea into your nature.

I know this without any doubt because I've experienced it. It's how I mastered becoming a personal trainer. It's how I mastered peak performance coaching. And it's how I mastered public speaking.

Thanks to those experiences, I'm totally confident that if I wanted to master, say, yoga, then I would need to dedicate my practice to it.

The same is true for you. If you genuinely want something, it needs to be your goal, and you need to be prepared to practice and pursue it over other aspects of your life. There's no point in being half-hearted about it and regretting never attaining your target.

On social media, I can't tell you how often I get asked, *Hey JP, please tell me how to be a speaker. How can I be a powerful and confident public speaker?* And my answer is always the same: *Get out there and start speaking!*

You're not going to learn by sitting on your sofa and looking at LinkedIn. You need to push yourself outside and start your journey. Yes, it may be uncomfortable at the beginning, and you may be embarrassed and feel like you're always making mistakes, but you must start your practice and accept that you won't appear on day one as a fully polished speaker. You will, though, be learning every time you stand up and open your mouth. You'll be normalising an act you may have been fearful of, and that will reduce your fear in time.

Stick with it. Turn an idea into practice that becomes nature to you.

That isn't complicated advice.

I'm not some sorcerer here to wave a magic wand in your direction or spray some magic dust over you. I haven't made a scientific breakthrough that enables me to share some hitherto unknown secret of the universe with you. What I'm able to do is tell you what has worked for me and what has worked time and time again for other successful people that I've surrounded myself with over the years. It's a tried and tested approach with a long history of positive results for those who commit to it.

So if you want something different in your life, take responsibility and dedicate yourself to the practice.

It's a proven route to mastery.

Later in this book, I'm going to share with you three areas of mastery. I'll discuss mastering your mind, your body and your heart. But before that, let me tell you how I came to understand the importance of those three areas myself. Let me tell you the story of the charity cycle challenge that changed my life.

JOGLE

In 2019, a friend and coaching client, Callum O'Brien, and I decided to raise money for a couple of charities that were very close to our hearts: The Brain Tumour Charity for me and Macmillan Cancer Support for Callum.

I wanted to support my cause in memory of the incredible Addie Brady, who had died the previous year aged just sixteen. Callum had lost his mum to cancer in 2018 and wanted some way to re-pay the support he received.

We're both people who want to set significant, stretching goals, so we settled on cycling between the northernmost point of the United Kingdom to the southernmost tip – from John O'Groats in the Highlands of Scotland to Land's End at the foot of Cornwall, England, or as it's often called by the acronym formed by its start and finish locations, JOGLE.

Because we wanted to make the challenge even more formidable, this route is traditionally seen as the 'wrong' way round. Most people undertaking the effort try to complete it from south to north, Land's End to John O'Groats – LEJOG.

That's because, under normal circumstances, the UK's weather is governed by the way the North Atlantic jet stream sweeps eastward and down towards continental Europe before pushing back up the length of the island. The prevailing wind tends to come from the south west, so cycling from that direction towards the north makes complete sense because the wind is generally pushing with you.

For JOGLE, it's mainly blowing into your face the whole way. The intensity junkies inside me naturally figured the hardest direction would be the better one. And to make it yet more challenging, we set ourselves the eye-catching target of extending the route so that we would complete 1,000 miles (1,609 km) in ten days.

We set off in May 2019. Everything was going perfectly to plan, and we were well on track. The ride had been largely uneventful which is, of course, precisely what we'd hope for. And then at the end of day seven, one of our team spots a small issue: 'Guys, I've just realised that we're going to have a bit of a problem. You've marketed this whole charity event as 1,000 miles in ten days, but if you stick to the route we've set out, you're going to be short of the target distance. We're kind of running out of miles.'

So over dinner that evening, we discussed a plan to *extend* the route.

Of course, we'd finished three-quarters of the ride by now, so we couldn't simply add on a few easy miles each day. We had to work out how to add the necessary distance to the final two days of our challenge. To be fair, we didn't think this would present too much of a significant difficulty for us. Obviously, it might mean cycling slightly longer days, but we were into the groove of it all by now and had managed the mileage pretty well for the most part. We felt we could handle a few extra hours.

We had, however, planned this route several months in advance, so for a week, we'd always known exactly where we were headed and where we would finish each evening. From now on, though, we'd have to explore an unexpected course. Callum and I studied the map, and eventually what appeared to be an obvious – and perhaps not unpleasant – new ride came into view. We agreed that rather than going straight through the middle of Devon, we would hug the county's northern coastline and include an additional semi-circle of miles onto our task. Maybe a couple days of coastal views would actually be a picturesque way to finish?

Wrong! What we hadn't accounted for was that the North Devon coast is most definitely not a flat, beachside ride or a consistent cliff-edge pedal. It is up, it is down and then it is up again. Rinse and repeat. The coast roads form an endless undulation of hill-upon-hill – like those images you see of mathematical sine waves.

It seemed never-ending. Until the start of our little detour, most days we had climbed off our bikes around 6 o'clock in the evening. That absolutely wasn't going to happen on this day. At around 6pm on day eight of the challenge, I messaged my wife at the time: 'Put in a prayer for me, this is going to be a long day. I don't think we're going to finish until about 8 o'clock tonight.'

After that message, there isn't much else about that day that I remember.

Crash

From here on in, I'm really just going by what others have told me since that day. My memory of that fateful evening has been wiped from my mind which, as I've suggested, is probably a blessing.

The last thing that I do recall happened just before 7pm…

…I pull over and flag down our support vehicle to stop alongside me. It's near the end of May, but there's no sign of any late-spring heatwave – the temperature hit 18°C (64°F) during the day; quite cloudy with only a light breeze to work against. I appreciate the weather because, given all the effort we'd put in climbing and descending all day, these are about as perfect conditions as we could hope for at this time of year.

Usually, we'd finish each day in good time, but because of our longer route today, we're still on the road at 7pm and expecting to be out for another hour or so. As a result, being that bit later in the day, a chill is beginning to gather in the air.

As it turns out, the mercury will drop to around 6°C (43°F) later that night. But I don't know that yet.

As I apply my brakes, I turn to Callum. 'You go ahead, and I'll catch up with you. I just want to grab my arm and leg warmers.'

Callum nods his approval and rides on as I slow down.

I never do catch him up.

The support van stops with me and I exchange a few idle pleasantries with Chris, our driver, as I fish out the warmers and put them on. Once I'm ready to continue, Chris, as he always does, sees me off, just to make sure I get back on the road safely. I've been grateful for that all week. It's a nice touch.

I reflect on a tough day. There have been times when I've wondered what I'm doing today, gasping up yet another steep road that seems to have no end. I curse the miscalculation that means we've had to alter the route at the last minute from our well-researched track cutting through the heart of Devon's countryside, and silently wonder to myself what our day would have been like had we followed that road. I picture a beautiful tarmac straight line. Pan flat and traffic free as we're cheered on by well-wishers lining the roadside. I picture already having had a warm shower. I picture tucking into a carb and protein-rich evening meal, celebrating being so close to the finish line. Instead, I am here, still out riding, feeling the fatigue in my legs and the stiffening ache from the curve in my back.

But, you know, it's not so bad. We're going to make it, that's not in doubt. We're going to have kept our promise to ride 1,000 miles in ten days. It's a lovely, cool evening for being out on the bike and this is a pretty part of the world. I am lucky. It could be so much worse for me. And I will have earned the meal I enjoy tonight more than ever.

My shoes 'click' as I clip my feet back into my pedals. Just one last push. I pick up some speed and crest yet another rise, but this time there's a nice drop to follow.

'Right JP, let's get moving and get back to Callum.'

It's a partnership. We help each other along, and it'll be good to coast to a stop for the day together. So no freewheeling down this slope for me.

'Get your head down and keep turning the pedals, JP.'

My breath's under control, and this is fun. I can feel the breeze forcing itself through the vents in the top of my helmet as I pick up speed, and the extra clothing I've just put on makes me feel warm and protected. It's the home straight. Nearly done. There is a sensation of freedom. I pedal without much resistance.

As it descends, the road curves around a long bend.

My fingers rest lightly on my brake levers, and I focus on the tarmac directly in front of my tyre. Just a couple of days till I'm back at home. I hear the roar of the wind rushing against me.

Everything's OK. I am in a good place.

And then... there is black.

◆

SERIOUS TRAFFIC COLLISION, ILFRACOMBE – CYCLIST SERIOUSLY INJURED

Police are investigating a collision in North Devon that has left one person with serious injuries.

At around 7:15pm on Wednesday 22 May, Police were notified of a serious collision on the A399 between Ilfracombe and Combe Martin involving a cyclist and a Ford Focus.

The rider of the pushbike, a 37-year-old man, was airlifted to Derriford Hospital with life-changing arm and leg injuries.

A 69-year-old man from Ilfracombe has been arrested on suspicion of dangerous driving, taking a vehicle without consent, driving whilst disqualified, and driving whilst unfit. He was later released under investigation pending further enquiries.

The road remained closed for eight hours to allow Roads policing officers and forensic collision investigators to attend and examine the scene.

Police are appealing for witnesses and would like to hear from anyone who witnessed either the pushbike or the vehicle prior to the collision or the impact itself.

Police would like to thank members of the public for their patience during the scene closure.

Devon & Cornwall Police

https://www.devon-cornwall.police.uk/News/newsarticle.aspx?id=98a1b016-cf78-453c-957c-f416b049b287

◆

As I understand it from the reports I've read and what I've been told by various people since, I was making my way down a curving hill with no problems when a driver – uninsured, unfit and in someone else's vehicle – came up the hill on the wrong side of the road, hit me head-on and simply carried straight on *through* me. As if I was a fly squished against his windscreen.

My bike snapped into around twenty pieces.

That's not what normally happens to bikes on impact in a collision.

Usually, the front fork breaks, and the rest of the frame absorbs the stress, so they get twisted and bent. Under the extreme force of my crash, the frame simply shattered into little pieces.

Later, as the days, weeks and months in hospital mounted, I would play a dark game with myself – trying to piece the bike together like a jigsaw from the photos I'd been given.

At the scene, around eighty to one hundred metres separated my resting place from my bike. I was off the road, starting to tumble down a bank, but appeared to have been stopped by a tree that prevented me falling further.

They found me lying wedged between the tree and a metal barrier.

Rescue

I stay lying there for about an hour and a half.

An air ambulance was called, but unfortunately, the helicopter can't reach me. Despite that seemingly gloomy wait, I also benefitted from some extraordinary good fortune too: the first person to stop is a paramedic; the second is an off-duty police officer and, incredibly, the third is someone from the Royal National Lifeboat Institution (RNLI) who just happens to have an oxygen tank in their car.

I wonder where I'd be now without the help of those three generous souls.

It's impossible for me to imagine that this fortunate procession of relevantly skilled, qualified and equipped passers-by wasn't meant to be.

I'm convinced that it was ordained so that I could

live to share my story, inspire more people and encourage audiences to relate to and connect with me. It's unquestionably the biggest challenge of my life, but I maintain – and this is still going to sound slightly bizarre to some of you – that it's honestly the best thing that's ever happened to me too.

Ninety minutes or so after I come to rest at the base of the tree, the paramedics are finally able to safely transfer me to a nearby field where the helicopter can land.

I am airlifted from the north coast of Devon to the south coast, sixty miles to Derriford Hospital in Plymouth, for two weeks in intensive care.

It is the beginning of a two-month stay in hospital.

If you're squeamish, then the next section might *not* be for you. *Perhaps skip the next couple of paragraphs.*

I break both my legs and an arm. Not minor, you-need-a-magnified-x-ray-to-see-it hairline fractures... but completely shattered, bone-sticking-right-out-of-the-limb breaks.

I snap my tibia twice and my fibula once.

I break my femur in half, and my leg is twisted around *behind my body.*

I snap my arm in three places.

But bones weren't the be-all and end-all: on top of the breaks I have a punctured and collapsed lung, trauma to my heart, and I need urgent surgery to repair my bowel.

I am in a pitiful state. It would have been no surprise to anyone if my life had ended beside the A399 or in the hospital ICU.

I only have one woozy, dream-like recollection of that period and it was of waking up to see my arm in what seemed to be a very odd position.

I remember thinking, *this is weird* that despite my best efforts, I couldn't move anything. I considered this situation, then fell back into a heavily sedated sleep.

What my team told me afterwards was that they were there at this point, and they could visibly see the life draining out of me.

While I am in intensive care, I am getting worse, not better.

My heart starts jumping around, beating erratically. I develop a severe chest infection. At one point, the medical staff have to find and attach a bigger oxygen mask for my face because I stop breathing.

Not long after this, one of the doctors said to me: 'You obviously have a very strong mindset. And you're lucky that you're so fit and healthy.'

And I thought: 'Oh, darn.'

◆

So why do you think you survived?

I'm here for a reason. And I owe it to myself and everyone else to go all-in on that. I think I had that accident because I was growing so fast that I couldn't see the truth.

So the universe put me on my ass. The universe made me stop.

Because I fully recognise that if I kept doing what I was doing, I might have achieved great things. I might have done many more fitness challenges and gone from a six-figure coach to a seven-figure coach.

But that's not why I'm here.

I love coaching. I'm damn good at coaching. I can rip you to pieces by going inside you and asking you the very best questions that will challenge you to the core and help you find out what's really going on and then help rebuild you from the inside out.

I run amazing events and all that stuff. But that comes very naturally to me.

I work with a few people a year through private coaching, run a mastermind coaching group, host a few events myself and speak at many other events.

But referring to the third part of life mastery – *heart/spirit mastery*, I realised there was *heart* missing. You can have the body and the mind, but why are you here?

It's not for the body, and it's not for the mind. It's for the impact that you create whilst you're here in your own existence. It's following your heart, living in your heart and serving from your heart.

So I thought, 'What is the heart for me?' It's care. It's truth. It's contribution.

And I thought, 'Wow! If I'm learning that what's *missing* from my life is the heart element, living for others and not for oneself. Then, actually, I think this is what other people might be missing, too.'

Even if you haven't quite mastered your body or your mind yet, if you live for others, you will always be *outside* of yourself, outside of your ego, and you won't be in depression, misery or suffering.

When you're focused on serving and helping other people, you don't focus on your own pain or suffering. But that unconditional love you end up giving to others is what then comes back to you!

My focus and determination through recovery were never about me. What pushed me through my recovery was, I knew that my recovery was for everyone.

Someone asked me recently, 'Why do you put everything on social media?' Because it's not for me, it's for the kid in Australia. It's for when his mother messages me and says, 'My kid is 12 years old, and he's got a physical disability. He watches your videos every single day. Thank you!' That's why I continue to do what I do and show up in my life the way that I do.

So I did it for everyone, and I documented everything for everyone.

Because I always had these stories of physical and mental habits, but I had never before been through a traumatic experience such as a near-death accident.

And most people probably know that some people hold on to a moment of trauma, and they let it define the rest of their life.

And I refuse to be like that. I refuse to live like that. I am fully 100% committed to showing that, regardless of whatever you've been through, you don't have to be a victim. You can come out victorious.

That was my obsession. I take two steps forward and one step back, but every time, I keep moving.

◆

Realisation

Why did I think, 'Oh darn,' at that moment?

Because the realisation suddenly struck me with full force: this is precisely what I've been practising for my whole life. This is it, the time when I can implement all the physical and mental strategies I've trained for, ingrained in my mind and turned into second nature.

That's what it's all been about.

It gives me goosebumps writing this now, and every time I think about it. I have to believe that events like these happen by design, and I'm so grateful to be able to have this opportunity to share with you the lightbulb moment of my life. The time when an experienced health professional told me that everything I've ever practised for in my life was a critical, contributing factor towards my recovery and towards my ability to come out the other side alive and intact.

When I finally understood that my commitment to betterment was part of saving my life.

'You obviously have a very strong mindset. And you're lucky that you're so fit and healthy.' That's what the doctor said to me, and I'm happy to repeat it.

Those few words woke me up. Galvanised me.

I truly believe that fitness is *life fitness*, and that fitness – both mental and physical – helped save my life on the evening of May 22, 2019 and in the weeks, months and years of rehabilitation that have followed.

I intend to shout about that for the rest of my life.

Of course, just like any other journey to self-improvement, the road to recovery since then was tough and littered with falls and setbacks. Every two steps forward appeared – at the time – to be accompanied by another step back. But I'm OK with that because I've kept the doctor's words in my mind, and I know what I must do to get better.

There have been some hard months, though.

There have been days when I've veered towards depression and needed to make good use of the toolbox of skills I've picked up over the years to stay on track. Through my practice, I've learned how to get past these sticky times. There's no one right answer I can give you, except that by building up your mental and physical resilience, you're empowering yourself for the future. The more resilient you become, the more tools are available to you.

In this case, though, the first concept I'd dig out of the toolbox pretty much every time was *personal responsibility.*

Because you see, no one is coming to save me. There's no knight in shining armour riding towards me from over the horizon, ready to slay the dragon that's laying me low and free me from the situation I find myself trapped in.

I might be overwhelmed with sympathy as people all over the world feel sorry for me, but as nice as it is to know there are people out there who have love for me, that isn't going to help me learn to walk again. It's on me.

Self-pity won't get you anything you've ever dreamed of.

So I needed to take control and do something personally to shake myself out of my own misery and suffering. And, thanks to all the practice I'd put in, that's precisely what I did for those first few, tough months.

First, when I was trying to cling to life in hospital, then beginning my recuperation on the ward followed by finally walking out of the door and heading home to start the long road to recovery.

I was committed to that idea of taking control, and my restoration was going brilliantly. So brilliantly, in fact, that five months after my accident, I recognised that although I was far from physically 100%, I was pretty much back to full speed again; working at maximum effort and doing as much as I ever did.

I'd pushed myself hard, and as usual, it had delivered impressive results. That's when another realisation hit me:

'JP, what are you doing? You're recovering from a serious accident, and you're back to full speed already. Slow down!' And that was backed up by a friend telling me, 'JP, you almost freaking died. Dude, just chill!'

That was when I figured out that I was just being driven by my old 'friend' *intensity* once again.

You see, as I said, what you practice turns into your nature, for better or for worse. And throughout my adult life, I'd been practising intensity.

But it wasn't helping me anymore.

Can Do

I'd become so accomplished at practising intensity that I had to accept it was now part of my nature.

So here's a great question that I was able to confront myself with, just like I confronted it when I was a young man DJing in Latvia and knew I had to turn my life around: *How do you get rid of something that's in your nature, but isn't serving you well?*

It's such an essential question for so many of us.

The answer?

You need to find a new 'nature' to install in its place. How do you install a new nature? You know the response to this one by now, right?

You practice!

Here's a couple of examples I'm often presented with either in-person or on social media. Do you recognise yourself in either of these?

'JP, no matter how much I want to, I just don't seem to ever be able to get fit.'

If this is you, be honest with yourself here – how often do you really practice? How consistently do you back up that practice and over what period of time?

Many people start off with fine intentions – signing up for a gym membership, buying all the gear and so on – but then after a while, the motivation slowly ebbs away. Perhaps, after a hard day's work, they find that it's a dark, wet evening, and the idea of stepping outside to train doesn't seem so appealing.

So maybe they suggest a takeout or a trip down the pub with a friend. Which, of course, can be an excellent thing to do – we all know the power of social connection. But they've 'opened the door' so that the next time that slight feeling of apathy strikes it's just that tiny bit easier to skip the training session again. Little-by-little, the practice fades away until they find themselves asking why they never seem able to get fit.

If that sounds familiar, don't feel bad. Everyone does it in one guise or another. But you need to be aware of it, and you need to take ownership for your actions, recognising that we make our own choices and priorities in life based on where we are and how we feel in that moment.

The other common question I get is: 'I hear people talk a lot about positivity, but you know what, I really struggle with being positive.'

My response is always to ask what that person is actually doing to try to promote positivity in their life.

Very often, they reply that they're going about their day as usual while trying to look on the bright side.

That won't ever be enough. Your brain is a muscle, and just like our quads, biceps or abs, it needs to be trained. Training means actively practising. Want to train your quads? Do some squats. Want to train your biceps? Lift some weights? Want to train your abs? Get on the floor and hit those sit-ups and planks.

Exactly the same principle applies for positivity of mind.

Take time to think about your life goals, write them down and set smaller milestones you know you can achieve. Cross them off as you go.

Keep a gratitude journal every single day, writing down all the good things – however small and insignificant they might seem – that have happened to you over the last 24 hours. Maybe someone made you a cup of tea, maybe you saw a butterfly outside, or maybe you finally cleaned the kitchen sink.

Write down your gratitude for all those things!

Don't forget to confront the day-to-day fears that inhibit your positivity either.

So often, negativity is born out of being afraid of something. You might be negative about meetings because you're worried about having to speak up, or negative about the future because you're focusing on all the bad stuff that could happen along the way, regardless of how likely it really is to turn out like that.

The first step is acknowledging this to yourself. Admit that these underlying reasons exist rather than suppressing your feelings and misdirecting your anger or resentment. Then ask yourself what you can do about it.

Do you need to start with a public speaking course and take the big leap to normalise the sensations of having the eyes of the room upon you? Do you need to find space for mindful meditation that can clear your mind?

Stick with it. It won't happen overnight, but science tells us that, as I keep saying, with practice, you can ultimately re-wire the neural pathways in your mind to think differently. If you simply ignore your fears and hope for the best, your negativity will not disappear.

I have a number of trigger words that, when I hear people say them, I instantly know there's a problem. For example:

- Try

- But

- No time

Those words are red flags telling me that someone isn't fully committed to the practice needed to change their life in the way that they say they want.

Are you only trying to practice something instead of actually doing it? If you would practice more but x, y or z keeps getting in the way, then what I hear is someone making excuses.

And do you often feel like you have no time to practice? Then I have to ask, 'Who is in control of your life?'

Because we all choose our priorities in life. Many of them are valid, but if something's really important to you – say, your kid's birthday or using that free ticket someone gave you to go to the World Cup Final (imagine that!) – you'd make enough time for it, right? So why can't you make time for practice if this is as important to you as you say it is?

The reality is some people just aren't willing to do the work.

And that's OK. I get that. If that's you, be at peace with it. You make your own decisions, so there's no point beating yourself up about something that, when push comes to shove, you're not prepared to put the effort in to achieve. Be kind and accepting of yourself.

In the same way that we're never going to attain a world where everyone is happy to consume food that's only made from plants, neither are we going to make all eight billion people on the planet positive thinkers. There is a balance of everything in this life – a yin to every yang.

While I can't change everyone, I can affect the balance that exists in the world, and that's what I've set out to do. Achieving that will be my legacy. It's a big, tough challenge, but it's also incredibly rewarding. Because part of the mental mastery I've developed has always been focused on helping you see what you can do as opposed to what you can't.

◆

You talked about how your accident changed your life. Has it affected your spirituality? Have you become more spiritual?

Yeah, I'm more spiritual.

I've done many talks now since my accident, and at every talk, at least one person has said to me, 'Your energy is very different.'

I've always wanted to make a massive impact – not in numbers but in change and transformation. I've always wanted to know that my life mattered; that my life meant something. And for a long time, I was unsure how I wanted to do that until I met one of my coaches, Lisa Nichols.

We spent five days together. I was telling her what I do. And she said, 'JP, you keep saying that you're transforming minds, you're transforming people, you're a high-performance coach. But when you say it, I just don't believe it. I don't feel it. You have a gift, and it's bigger than what you're saying. You aren't here to transform minds. You're here to heal hearts.'

Umph! I needed to hear that, but it was uncomfortable. All I've ever taught is what I've practised in my own life. And all I've ever done, I've done for myself first and then shared it with others. My biggest 'goal' in my life is to heal my own heart because of everything that I've been through.

I thought, 'Damn! How am I gonna heal hearts?' That felt uncomfortable even saying it to people.

I was the guy always in a tailored suit, and I was thinking, 'My corporate clients and my business associates are going to think JP has frickin lost the plot, man. He's gone all woo-woo. It must be all the VEGAN FOOD!'

And then, when I lay in hospital, I had that moment of realising that I'm already doing it. I just didn't understand what I was doing or why I was here. I was doing it to my full potential based on what I believed I could do, which was 'I can *transform* your mind.' But I didn't think I had the ability to *heal* someone.

And then two weeks after spending time with my coach, I ran an event in London. People who were there at that event would agree that there were hearts healed in that room. After that event, I went up to my hotel room and just cried because I accepted who I was becoming. Seeing the impact I was having on others was beautiful and almost unreal.

So yes, I'm more spiritual, but not because I want to be seen as more spiritual or to be perceived in any different way. It's just that I want to engage with people's hearts, and I think I needed to.

Doing that meant coming down a step from my high-performance platform. I've proved everything that I need to prove. I don't need to prove anything to anyone anymore. I've done it! I've done the ultra-marathons, spoken all over the world, been a pro fighter, had the fancy toys. I've done it all. Now it's time for me to come down and calm down so that I can start to invite people in that previously wouldn't be able to come close to me because I was so intense and even, I'm told, intimidating. So I can help them heal their hearts and lives, just like I've done with mine.

◆

Celebrate

During my recovery, when I was walking around to rebuild my strength and perhaps gingerly attempting to climb down a few steps, I wasn't thinking, 'Oh man, I could have jumped off that with my eyes closed before. Look at me now!' That's self-defeating.

There's no point in looking backwards and being downcast about what you were once capable of. The only moment that matters is this one right now, and what you're trying to achieve in that moment is the only important factor. So instead of thinking, 'Woe is me,' my mind is instead reinforcing the positive message of my genuine achievement: 'Yes! I just walked down the stairs without holding on to the handrails! There's no way I could have done that a few weeks ago.'

Back in the hospital, when I first got up and started trying to walk – which was about six or seven weeks after the accident – the medical staff would say to me, 'JP, we're going to start getting you to try to walk.'

At this time, I was still in real trouble, physically.

My breaks are so bad that the surgeons need to take me back into the operating theatre and – with apologies to anyone who doesn't enjoy these kinds of visual descriptions of medical procedures – they open up my knee and drove a titanium rod through the centre of my bone all the way down to my ankle. The rod is then locked in place with screws at the ankle as if the surgeons were industrial repairmen fixing a piece of machinery.

That was part one.

Part two is to put another titanium rod in through my hip joint and all the way down my femur.

In case you're wondering, yes, it was sore, to say the least. But still, never mind Iron Man – he's last year's best superhero – I'm now the real Iron (Titanium) Man.

Anyway, after six weeks, the doctors say to me: 'Your bones are now healing around the metal, so let's start trying to get you to walk.'

It was good news that they thought I was now ready to begin, but, of course, it was daunting too. I hadn't walked anywhere since the day of the crash.

Slowly, the medical team help me get up, and I stand up. Imagine what it's like to stand up for the first time in so long, and when your body is still under such incredible stress. It's a unique and strange sensation.

The nurses in rehab bring over this black contraption – I don't know what it's called – a motorised, high-end physiotherapy mobily frame – that I had to lean on, and it holds me up and supports me because I am not capable of fully supporting myself to even stand on my own, despite all the weeks that I'd passed in that hospital.

A nurse presses a button on the device, and, slowly, it begins to raise me upright. So I'm standing there, but I'm really at the mercy of this strange black walking machine. There's virtually no weight at all going through my legs: this is really just about remembering the motion of walking at this stage, about getting my legs moving forwards and backwards.

'Are you ready?'

'Yeah, I'm ready.'

I take one step. Pause. I take one step. Pause. I take one step and pause again.

And this is how it goes, for the few metres of 'walking' across the room that I'm challenged with on that day.

It takes seemingly forever just to shuffle a few supported steps. And it's hard, you know. I've been a boxer, a cyclist, I've completed Ironman triathlons and all sorts of other extreme physical challenges, but these few steps are among the very hardest things I've ever attempted.

I take a deep breath in and a deep breath out.

'Are you good?'

'Yeah, I'm good. Let's go.'

Take a step. Take a step. Take a step...

My goal is to reach the chair in my room, and when I make it, the staff helps me to sit down. As soon as my backside hits the chair seat, I raise my arms into the air in triumph. 'Yes!'

I cried, and I celebrate as if I've just won an ultramarathon in a new world record time.

That was my life for longer than I care to remember: trying to get stronger at walking from my bed to my chair, over and over again.

Each time I did, it was cause for celebration.

When I eventually came home, the determination and the ultimate emotion didn't change one bit. My wife at the time, Julia, will tell you that when I managed to climb the stairs in our home, I'd celebrate. When I could climb down the stairs at home – which, let me tell you, is even harder than going up – I'd celebrate. And when I could climb up the stairs using just a single crutch? Go wild; it's time to celebrate!

I believe that it's vital to look for and give yourself as many opportunities to celebrate as possible every single day. The more you focus on these incredible positive achievements that you might otherwise treat as simple day-to-day events that you soon forget about, the more you're reinforcing a positive mindset. And reinforcement leads to the development of habits – good or bad.

If you go back to the first paragraph of this chapter, you'll see that I had a choice. I could have sat there in the hospital and thought, 'Woe is me,' but instead, I concentrated on goals that did me a world of good, both physically and mentally.

Now don't get me wrong, I'm a real human being just like you are. There are occasionally times when it's more of a challenge to view things in this way, but I don't let that define me and neither should you. For me, that glass really is 'half-full', and I'm thinking about what I can do with it rather than what I could have done with the half that's missing. I focus on what's in front of me – what I know I'm able to achieve – and I see the potential in everything as opposed to fixating on any of the failures I've been through or all the 'bad' things that have happened to me. Because what would be the point in that? What would I gain apart from sadness or bitterness or inertia in my life? You can practice this too if you'll only try.

◆

How do you overcome setting your goals too high and then not being able to fulfil or accomplish those goals?

First of all, I always remember that I'm the one setting the goals. So if I'm disappointed, it's because of myself, and I need to re-evaluate my goals.

Secondly, I always say, 'Make your goals uncomfortable, but don't make them unachievable.'

A lot of people are trying to achieve so much in a year or trying to achieve so much in three months. But actually, a lot of the times when I say to them, 'This is where you are now, this is where your goal is, whether you could get there in a year or three months, would that still be progress for you?'

'Yeah, definitely. Because right now, I'm here.'

So I ask, 'Would a year still be uncomfortable for you? Would that still require you to step up and become someone new?' More often than not, the reply is, 'Yes.'

A lot of times, we get excited or inspired; we go to a seminar, and we set these crazy goals. But then the gap between where we are now and getting there is too big.

So the third thing I would say is to remember goals and milestones. I said before 'celebrate everything'.

Obviously, my goal in my recovery was to get back to being fit. I mean the accident happened in May 2019, when I'd just cycled 860 miles over eight days across the UK against the wind, I'd done two amateur boxing fights in the same year – one Thai boxing and one standard boxing – and I'd run thirty-six miles from Rugby to Birmingham with a thirty-pound backpack on my back to speak at an event. I'd done a lot of great things, and my goal was obviously to get back to that.

But can you imagine if I just had that as my goal at a time when I couldn't even walk? How sorry would I feel for myself?

So I set milestones in place, and I would say, 'This is my goal for next year. In the next month, this is what I'd like to achieve.'

Set your big goal, your scary goal, and then reverse engineer it backwards: 'Okay, I think I'd like to achieve that goal in three years or five years or ten years.'

Then ask yourself, 'Where would I need to be one year

from now for me to know that I'm comfortably on my way to that goal?'

And then you reverse engineer again: 'Where would I need to be three months from now, to know that I'm comfortably, without any doubt, on my way to achieving my one-year goal?'

And then you can even go and break it into one month or one week.

Here's why this works so well: because if you now achieve your one-week goal, your mind is telling you that you're on your way to your big goal. How easy is it to achieve weekly goals?

It's much easier than achieving massive goals. I've used this for over a decade.

◆

Waking Up

Since the day of my accident – or more specifically, since the day I *woke up* as a different person, as the new, calmer and more collected version of my old self – there have been three powerful areas of focus in my life that I've been concentrating on.

I'm going to share them with you throughout the following chapters.

One reason I was able to make such a big mental switch was that, in the immediate aftermath of my crash and hospitalisation, I was empowered by the enormous outpouring of love I received from right around the world. That wave of love that broke over me truly affected my outlook and made me understand that all the chasing I'd been doing could finally stop. Because you see, in common with so many of you out there, all I ever wanted from a young age was a good life filled with love. That was the basic condition that I craved, and that drove me to want to make an impact and a difference in the world and to the lives of others.

I could have articulated that to you when I was just ten years old. At that age, I was a whisker away from being placed into foster care. It really was touch and go, and I'll never know how that would have changed the direction of my life.

While all of that turmoil to decide my future was going on, I sat down next to a homeless man, an African man in his eighties, and I gave him my sandwich.

In the scale of the totality of life on our planet, that might seem like the tiniest, most insignificant gesture, but to the two of us sat there at that moment, it was the biggest thing that could have happened, not least because that sandwich was my only food for the day.

I sat there with him while he ate it.

Obviously, I know that sandwich was important to the man at the time, but it's been important to me from that moment on. From that simple act of giving, I knew that from then on, I wanted to find ways to help others. I had no sense at all of what shape that might take – how I could possibly go about turning this feeling into a reality – only that there was something vital about helping other people and that I needed to keep doing it.

And so that short interaction coupled with the totality of the rest of my experiences during a rollercoaster childhood led me to spend most of my twenties and thirties chasing things, striving. I was determined that I wanted to get a good life, that I wanted to have as much love into my life as possible, and that I wanted to make as significant an impact as I could on the world around me. Man, I worked hard to achieve those goals. At many times, they were all-consuming passions that I pursued relentlessly, 24/7.

Then I had the accident, and as I lay there in my hospital bed battling to survive, I found myself constantly bombarded – *bombarded* in the most positive and amazing way – by seemingly thousands of people all over the globe sending me their love, making and re-making connections with me, contributing their time, energy and money, and expressing their gratitude to me for the impact I'd made on their lives in the past.

That's when it struck me: 'Oh my God, I don't need to keep striving anymore. I've done what I set out to achieve.'

Up until that point, I'd constantly been moving so fast, pursuing my ambition, that I'd failed to take the time to stop and appreciate where I already was in my life. I simply couldn't, as the saying goes, see the wood for the trees.

In my mind, that period was like being on one of those super-fast bullet trains, rocketing along at 250mph the whole time. You're moving so fast that there's no way of seeing what's happening around you, and you definitely can't appreciate everything that exists outside the carriage you're riding in. You're living your life in a blur, and that definitely isn't leading your best life.

◆

And how hard is to change? Because presumably there's an element of ego in all of our past lives. How do you then get rid of that ego to adopt spirituality and healing?

That's a great question. Absolutely 100% there's ego. The short answer to that is to ask really good questions.

I'll be going backwards and forwards: ego, truth, ego, truth. One of my favourite words, and what I've become known for standing for, is *truth*.

Lisa Nichols says: 'Your life is the dash between your birth date and your death date on your gravestone'. And if I were to put one word on my headstone, I'd want everyone to know without any doubt that what I stood for was the truth.

So that's what brings me back out of ego and into God, or into the Universe: connection to truth and why I'm here. I'm here to serve others by sharing my truth.

Now, it might hurt you, it might hurt me, it might be uncomfortable, but it's why I'm here. So as soon as my ego kicks in and says, 'Hey, but everyone knows you like this or like that,' or, 'You've spent so much time building this career, why change it?', I always ask myself, 'Is this my authentic truth?' I can't hide from the answer.

I wake up, and I say, 'Why am I here? What am I doing today? Is this in alignment with what I want to do?'

Because I could quite easily say, 'Yay, me! I want to heal hearts! I found my purpose!', and then four weeks later realise that I've been so busy doing 'my thing' that I haven't actually done anything in that direction. So in a way, I check myself before I wreck myself.

As often as possible.

◆

Best Life

◆

What's next? And what's your legacy? What do you want to leave behind?

I believe that everyone deserves education and inspiration. Everyone deserves to have a mentor or a role model.

I have the most amazing online coaching community in the world. I have a Mastermind Coaching community called LIV100. We have people from different countries in this community who all support each other and encourage each other, and I just want to keep growing that.

And then as we grow it, we can start to create communities in each city where the LIV100 community members can connect with each other. The need for connection is the basis of our human existence. I want to give people access to that in the healthiest, happiest and most powerful way possible.

We all have basic human needs.

The number one need that every single human being has

above everything else is *connection*. And if you don't have connection, you'll fall into *addiction*, and you'll fall into misery and suffering.

I love natural living, and if you look at any natural tribe in the whole world, whether in the Amazon, the bush, the jungle, the Arctic regions or wherever, the worst thing you can do to a human being is to abandon them from their own tribe.

I want as many people as possible in the world to know that you don't have to be alone. Because in the world that we live in today, it's so easy to find support, connection and community coaching. It's just too easy to miss out.

There's always a way to get help, whether it's Narcotics or Alcoholics Anonymous, counselling, friendship or coaching – be it online or offline – there's always a way for you to move forward. But you'll never move forward unless you do that one thing that I mention in mental mastery, which is to *take responsibility.*

I'm not saying don't blame other people for what you've been through. I'm saying don't give them permission to control the rest of your life. Because your past doesn't define your future. So that's my legacy. I want to connect with as many people as possible and help them thrive because there are three ways in which you can live life: suffer, survive or thrive. Surviving isn't living; it's just existing. And I hope that for everyone who ever comes into contact with me that I can help them thrive in some way.

◆

Getting put on my ass in the hospital – with nowhere to go and nothing really to do except look out the window at the sky beyond – gave me the time and space to slow down and evaluate the most significant aspects of my life.

Gazing out of that window, feeling the love of all the people I'd come into contact with over my life (as well as that given by countless people I've still never met), it became clear to me that I'd already done what I'd set out to do.

Now was the time for me to both slow down and step up. I'd been given an opportunity to reinvent myself so that I could reach even more people. So that the true meaning of that one donated sandwich wouldn't get lost in the blur of everything I was doing but would instead be the front and centre of my attitude. In that sterilised room, surrounded by machines, connected to tubes, covered in bruises and scars from head to toe, I began to reimagine everything that I've ever taught and to appreciate that I was already living my best life.

I used the time to think deeply about everything that I was doing and everything that, since the age of ten, I'd always done, and now I want to pass that learning on to as many people as I can.

That's why I've brought it all together and established LIV100.

As the name suggests, it's about living your values 100% so that you can *live your best life.*

I've already explained how: by repeatedly practising positive intentions and behaviours, you can achieve much more than you ever thought was possible. Similarly, if you continue to repeat negative thought patterns and actions, you'll reinforce that negativity, and it'll creep into every area of your life.

If you stick at the tasks and approach that I outline in LIV100, I promise that you will be able to reinvent yourself into the image of the person you want to be. Not only that, but you can do it time and time again as your requirements dictate.

Let me introduce you to the three fundamental pillars of LIV100:

- Mind

- Body

- Heart

I'll explain more about each of the in turn throughout the remaining three chapters.

Mind

When I talk about Mind, I'm referring specifically to attaining mental mastery. I break this endeavour down into four separate, simple components.

Responsibility

The easiest way to describe this is by working through the example from my own life that triggered everything:

I have always taken full responsibility for the accident.

Never to this day, not once, have I blamed the driver for what happened on that road in Devon one Spring evening in May 2019. I have no reason to.

Yes, I believe that for the sake and safety of other road users he shouldn't be on the road, but I must take responsibility for the choices I made to be there at that minute on that day. I chose to undertake the charity ride. I chose to alter the route of that day's effort. I chose to stop and put on my arm and leg warmers just moments before the car sped up the road and hit me. That's how it was.

Otherwise, how far back should you go with that 'what if?' process?

I was where I was because I chose to do the charity cycle challenge in May 2019.

I was where I was because I chose to do a charity cycle challenge in the first place.

I was where I was because I chose to do a challenge with my client.

I was where I was because I chose to work with my client.

I was where I was because I chose to have a coaching business.

Seriously, how far back should you go? All the way to sitting down beside a homeless man and giving him my sandwich as a ten-year-old boy? Perhaps all the way back to the first creatures that climbed out of the swamp and onto land?

The more you think about it, the more ridiculous it gets not to take responsibility. If any one of those things hadn't happened in that way, if I'd made one or a thousand different choices, I may have written a different story for myself. And who knows what ending that story might have had?

We often assume after something bad has happened that there could not have been a worse outcome, but with so many possibilities open to us, we have no idea what the result might have been.

All I know is that I take responsibility for my actions and that this path has presented me with an incredible opportunity to re-evaluate and re-focus my true purpose in life. That's why I always make myself responsible for me – and so should you.

People

Allied to taking responsibility is making sure that the right people surround you to allow you to move forward positively and appropriately.

The people I have in my life have been immensely valuable to me.

During my recovery, I made a point of thinking about who I genuinely needed around me at that time. I wanted to ensure that the space around me was filled with those who could enable me to progress and that I wasn't exhausting myself by using up energy on those who might not facilitate my development in the same way. That doesn't mean that I don't like or have no time for the people who weren't around my bed as I recovered, just that you have to make priorities for your own sake depending on the particular set of circumstances you find yourself in.

When you surround yourself with the right people for the goals you've chosen to target, you can think of this group as a 'breakthrough boardroom'.

You're the CEO of your life. The buck stops with you. So when you need to make a critical decision, you want to be able to walk into a boardroom filled with only the right people who can help you make the best decision. The people in that boardroom will change depending on the type of decision you need to make. If you have a problem with finances, you'll want a team of finance gurus in the room. If you have a problem with personnel, you'll want to hear from your HR experts. So ask yourself for each goal or stage in your life: who would you want to be with you in that boardroom to make the big, *eureka* breakthrough that might change everything for the better? When you imagine being surrounded only by that dream team, there may not be room for every single person in your life.

But of course, that doesn't mean the line up won't change in future.

So your specific boardroom can reflect both short and long-term priorities.

The point is, you need to give its composition some attention and not just hope the right people show up to save you at the right time. Remember what I just said about taking responsibility, right?

For me, I thought about who I needed in my breakthrough boardroom to help me get through my recovery as quickly and as fully as possible. I consciously chose the people who I felt I needed to immerse myself in. I spent time with them in-person, on the phone or messaging them from the confines of my hospital bed. I spent time watching their videos, reading their books, listening to their audiobooks and podcasts, and they all helped me through what could have been an incredibly tough time in anyone's life. They all helped me restore myself and get better more quickly.

Unless you've been in a similar situation and surrounded yourself with a robust support crew as I did, it's hard for me to explain just what a substantial difference it makes.

One of the major factors, though, is a straightforward

one: you're not alone. Instead, you're collaborating with other, helpful people in a shared goal, acting as a united force.

Never underestimate the strength of togetherness and connection you gain from being with your fellow humans. Whereas if you're alone, you're unsupported and are much more likely to suffer. It's not rocket science, but it's amazing how often people retreat and withdraw from their networks at times of hardship when it's precisely the opposite that they need. So be sure to find people around you who can help you go on a collective journey from suffering, surviving and just 'getting by' to people who are flourishing and thriving.

Meaning

Meaning, purpose, call it what you will.

Whatever name you give it, it's vital that you have one to work towards. Otherwise, what's all this effort for? You must have a direction, and that direction needs to have some relevance to you. There's no point in setting yourself a target that you have no passion for and which doesn't provide you, anyone or anything else with some form of benefit.

In my personal example, I created a positive meaning for myself and my life, and then I went to work on it. I made a non-negotiable commitment to form a positive meaning out of an intense experience I'd been through. Then I promised to invest myself fully in working towards my goals with that meaning always foremost in my mind.

So I started to think, and I started to write, and I started to speak that meaning into existence. Although it was a traumatic event followed by a long, hard road to recovery, there's no question that this was the most brilliant thing that had ever happened to me in my life. It's up to you to find the positive meaning in your own existence and to use it as your mind's spirit guide through the ups and downs of being a human as you aim for your ultimate goals.

What's your next move?

Having taken responsibility, surrounded myself with the right people and established a positive meaning for my life, it was time to ask, 'What's next?'

The phrase *What's your next move?* is never far from my mind, literally – I wear a baseball cap with the initialism WYNM printed on the front. It's a strong message to keep reminding yourself and others of it.

It wasn't a new idea for me.

The old, ultra-intense version of myself was just as committed to that concept as I am today. Prior to the accident, I would have said something like, 'I don't care what you did yesterday. I only care about what you do next.' It really does matter. You can't bask in the reflected glory of some previous achievement forever. How long before that wears thin? If someone said, 'Good job' to you this morning, how long could you trade off of that one example of better-than-expected work? A day? A month? A year? Ten years? There comes a point when your achievement, whatever it was, is going to be yesterday's news, so you're only going to be as good as whatever you aim for and achieve tomorrow.

There's a phrase in the arts world, usually applied to musicians and bands: *one-hit wonders*.

It's never said as a compliment. It's always intended as a slight against a career that didn't achieve its full potential. A career that had its single, firework moment and then never hit the heights again.

Not solely reserved for musicians, there are plenty of one-hit wonders in the rest of the world too: people who attain some form of success once and then expect to be able to live off the profit – financial or otherwise – of that one thing for the rest of their lives.

It rarely turns out that way.

Even Steve Jobs had to do a bit more than simply come up with the first Apple computer. He had to find its market, listen to feedback, come up with new versions, refine the design, launch the iPod, the iPhone and the iPad, and so much more. If he'd stopped at the first Apple Mac, he'd be a historical side-note with a quirky looking machine kept in an obscure museum somewhere.

You have to be thinking about your next move all the time.

Look at The Beatles. Between 1962 and 1970, they recorded something like three hundred songs. Around two hundred of those were released at the time, nearly forty of which reached the UK Top 40. That's jaw-dropping.

It's not like all two hundred songs were put out as singles – some of them were album tracks (and by the way, their albums have spent over 1,000 weeks in the UK charts – a total of twenty years!). That's because the band and their management team always thought about the next move. It was a constant process of creativity. During that stellar period, they didn't once lean back in their comfy armchairs, put their hands behind their heads and contentedly pronounce, 'Ahh, that *Love Me Do* is a great song. We're set for life. I think we'll call it quits now and see how far we can ride that horse.' No! They kept going. They kept trying to uncover the magic over and over again, and they blessed us with an impressive and highly influential catalogue of music.

Always looking for the next move is a crucial part of mind mastery, and in my hospital bed and beyond, I was continually doing just that.

In fact, I've already told you about the moves that I took next: my first tentative steps to the chair across the room, graduating to using crutches without the physical support that held me upright, walking up and down stairs on my own and then without the crutches at all.

For months – years, even – focusing on my next move has been central in my mind, and almost all I've done. And as I do it, I realise that it's exactly what I've been doing pretty much all my life. It's one of the critical success factors that's got me to where I am today.

Body

Body refers to *physical mastery*.

You should look after your body – as the saying goes, *you only get one of them so use it wisely.* But for anyone trying to live their best life, being in optimum physical condition is an extremely important element of success. To help you understand exactly what I mean by physical mastery, I've split it into two main sections: *Stretch Goals* and *High Performance Habits*.

Stretch Goals

While the physical act of stretching is undoubtedly an essential part of any fitness regime, it is, of course, not what I mean here.

Stretch yourself beyond the expectations you have for your day-to-day capabilities.

Please, always have something in your life to work towards. Set yourself a physical goal that is so scary, so uncertain and so uncomfortable that just by signing up to the challenge it forces you to become something more than you already are.

And go public with it too. Tell your friends, your family, your social networks – tell everyone you know – that this is the journey you're on and that you have a big, bold endpoint in mind. There's nothing more likely to commit you to following something through than knowing that the eyes of the world are upon you.

Perhaps you know the feeling in the pit of your stomach when, for example, you've gone online and paid the entrance fee for your first marathon. It can be a scary kind of *Oh no!* sensation. A heady mix of excitement, terror and just sheer bewilderment at the amount of effort you're going to have to invest in getting from where you are now to where you know you'll need to be on that date in a few months' time. And yet, in that simple act of commitment – paying an entrance fee to confirm your place – you're turning something that once seemed totally impossible into something that now seems almost within reach.

You know it's going to take plenty of hard work to get there, but you now have a goal and a pathway to achieve it.

And every time you go through this process of turning the seemingly impossible into the possible, you get a little bit closer to realising your full potential. This is especially true once you start attaining these once-unreachable targets that you set for yourself. At that point, you fully understand that you can push yourself that little bit further than you previously thought. The more you do it, the more it becomes self-evident that the limits you used to set were only in your mind.

Your full potential is unlimited – if only you would try to stretch yourself.

High-Performance Habits

Don't *pretend* that you have achieved physical mastery.

I'm not talking about rock-hard, six-pack abs or washboard stomachs – whatever you want to call it – I'm talking about *energy*.

Without energy and your commitment to good health, the game's over before it has even started.

How do you give yourself energy? By cultivating high-performance habits. Not habits like, 'Oh, you know what, it's a beautiful sunny day today, I think I'll go out for a jog,' or 'Ah, it looks like I've got fifteen minutes spare before my favourite TV programme starts, perhaps I'll squeeze in a little meditation.'

That's almost the opposite of a habit. That's making excuses for all the other days that you don't feel like getting up from the couch.

No, habits are like commandments: *I shall not*, or *I absolutely will*. They are non-negotiable guarantees to yourself that you will definitely do something on a regular basis come rain, shine, birthdays, work chaos, nights out or just general lethargy. They are unshakeable, unmissable events in your daily calendar, and you're cheating yourself if you make excuses not to do them.

Habits form over time, and they get easier with practice. You might start something – say a daily run – with great enthusiasm and energy. But eventually, that honeymoon period will fade away. You'll be laying in your bed in the dead of winter, thinking about how your improvements have started to wane, and how you thought you might have felt a little ache in your foot the last time you went out, and you'll have reached a decision point: 'Do I get up and go outside in the cold and rain, or do I shut my eyes and enjoy this nice warm duvet for another thirty minutes?'

This is a test of whether you've developed a high-performance habit or not.

If you stay in bed, then you've cheated yourself. If you get up, then you're *reinforcing* that habit, and honestly, the mental and physical benefits you'll gain over time from making positive decisions like that are like rocket fuel for your best life.

As I said a moment ago, make sure you share your targets and milestones with friends.

If you struggle for self-motivation when it comes to getting going with physical activities, then knowing that your network is likely to keep enquiring about your progress is an extremely potent motivational force. It's a great way of encouraging the development of non-negotiable high-performance habits.

With all this talk of exceptional goals and reaching for the stars, I need to add an important caveat: *remember that you can only change your life one day at a time.*

Don't set your ambition to become an astronaut in thirty days' time, for example, because posting a single goal that's so wild without any steps along the way is merely setting yourself up for failure.

Also, don't forget that different targets are variably meaningful for different people.

You've already seen that there was a time when my aim was simply to shuffle a few steps across a hospital room while being held up by mechanical support. At that time, I had no thoughts of Ironman triathlons or climbing Mount Kilimanjaro, as I've done since. I just needed to put one foot in front of the other. Your target could be anywhere on the scale as long as it's relevant and ambitious for you.

It doesn't have to be complicated, but you need to make the commitment. You need to be ready to say, *Today is my day to change my life*, and know that you mean it not just in that moment but henceforth and forever.

There's also something fantastically liberating about saying that phrase out loud. Because, you know what, one day you're going to fail. It's OK, we all do it and we always will. But what's liberating is knowing that after you mess up for whatever reason, the next day you have an opportunity to get out of bed and once more say, *Today is my day to change my life*, and off you go again.

The more you practice with purpose, the better you'll get.

Practice may not necessarily make perfect, but it's an unavoidable fact that it makes you better and, ultimately, turns a distant ambition into reality and good habits into second nature.

◆

Talking about practice, you recently went on a Vipassana silent meditation retreat. Tell us more about that?

Vipassana is known as the closest thing to living like a monk or a nun.

It's Buddhist teachings, and traditionally it starts as a ten-day experience. It's not a religious ritual; it's a meditation practice. You live in a Buddhist meditation centre for ten days in complete silence. But ten days wasn't enough for me, so I signed up to two different retreats – one was six days, and the other was ten days – and I was accepted onto both. There was a single-day gap in between.

Vipassana basically involves meditating and living in complete silence; no gestures to anyone, no writing, no reading, completely no distractions outside of yourself. That silence forces you to go *inside.*

All human beings have the ability to focus their attention and intention on two areas: *outside* or *inside* of us.

And most of us live our lives with all our attention and intention *outside* of ourselves – in the traffic, at work, at home, with our families, on the commute, and so on.

So in Vipassana, by removing every single thing that could possibly *distract* you *outside*, you're forced from morning till night to focus on the truth of what's happening *inside* you.

I did sixteen days of living in silence, meditating for ten to twelve hours a day, drinking water, eating vegan food and keeping my mouth shut the rest of the time."

What did you find out about yourself?

I got a lot of reminders.

Also, what was really great was that when I came out of the hospital, I told everyone that I have no animosity or feelings towards the driver that hit me. But I'm so resilient by nature, that when I was able to stop and remove everyone, I didn't have to prove how strong I am.

On day two of this silent experience, I just broke down in tears, and I got really angry. It was just still there, and it needed to come out.

I had a lot of confirmation that I'm here to serve. I'm here to heal hearts. I got a lot of clarity.

And then that moment for me was epic: 'Oh, wow, I do *feel* some stuff.' It wasn't until I stopped my busy life that I was actually able to *feel* what was really going on inside and let it all go.

It lasted for about an hour. I just cried and was angry, and then just kind of hung my head for the rest of the day and took some deep breaths. Then I thought, 'Cool, I'm glad I got that's out now.'

I was ready to let it go. The clarity that I got was insane.

And I felt like every day, as it became more and more difficult, I felt like I was becoming more and more powerful to the point that on about day twelve or thirteen when only three days were remaining, I could feel the energy outside of this piece of land we were having the retreat on. And I could feel the energy of the nearby cities, London and the UK, and it just felt so incredibly chaotic to me and delusional and unnecessary.

I looked beyond the trees into nothing, and I knew why I was here. I know why I'm here. I could feel it. I could feel everything. I felt like I myself was just energy and connected to the entire universe.

◆

Heart

◆

We're so blessed that you chose to stay after your terrible accident. But if you hadn't made it, and you were at the pearly gates, who would you have chosen to share the stage with you in paradise?

That's a really good question.

My first answer is Buddha. I would have loved to share a stage with a truly enlightened individual. I would have also loved to share a stage with Prophet Mohammed, Jesus Christ and some modern day spiritual teachers. People who lived their lives for others, who lived in service, and who live their lives with their hearts beaming right open. People who lived to LOVE… and loved to LIVE.

◆

The third and final side of the *Mastery Triangle* is *Heart*. I'm talking about mastery of the heart.

This is a big, emotional topic encompassing concepts like obsession, passion and purpose, but in essence, the best advice I can give you is concise, straightforward and easy to comprehend: *don't make your life all about you.*

It's such a revelation when you change your life from being one that is selfish and self-centred.

Believe me, I'm not attacking anyone here, but even those people who regularly give time to their community or money to their favourite charities or vote for political parties that care for others inevitably still hold on to some form of self-centredness in their daily lives. It's not anyone's fault. No one's to blame. That's simply the way society is, and we're hard-wired to put ourselves first.

We did it when we lived in caves, and we still do it now.

Let me promise something to you.

If you make your life, your mission, your career, your business, your family – everything in your conscious world – not about you, I promise that it'll motivate you more than you could ever imagine. It'll inspire you to get out of bed, get out of hospital, get out of misery and get out of suffering. Because although you may not realise it when you're in the depths of personal gloom, misery and suffering are all about you and your attitude.

No one else.

Whatever is going on in your life, the misery and suffering that you're feeling are created and fuelled by you.

If you stop looking inwards and stop focusing on your needs and start looking outwards and focusing on the needs of others, you'll invoke a formidable change that releases you from your personal challenges.

Live your life in the service of others.

Ever since the day I gave away that one little sandwich to a homeless man when I was ten years old, I've done my very best to follow that advice every day of my life, and in recent times, since my accident, I've made a special effort to double down on that intention.

It's incredible how you can re-frame and re-energise your own life by making the active decision to dedicate yourself to the people, animals and nature around you.

There are eight billion of us on this planet. Imagine the things we could achieve if we all stopped thinking about what we need to get out of life for ourselves and instead thought about what we could contribute to life on Earth, all together and for each other, as an eight-billion-strong collective? It gives me goosebumps just thinking about it.

Once you have mental and physical mastery as your base, you can go on to become the Leader to the world that you truly wish to be. I guarantee that once you have all of this under your control, you will be leading your very best life.

Postscript

◆

Have you forgiven the driver?

There are court cases going on.

It's not necessary for me to go to court, but I requested the court date. I want to see if I really have forgiven him. I think I have, but I want to put myself in an uncomfortable position to see if I really have. And if I come out of there, and I haven't forgiven him… then I've got more work and healing to do.

◆

March 2020

'DANGER DRIVER' SOZZLED IN COURT

Daily Star

**MAN APPEARS AT COURT 'TOO DRUNK'
TO ENTER PLEA**

North Devon Gazette

PENSIONER DENIES INJURING CHARITY CYCLIST IN CRASH WHICH BLOCKED MAJOR ROAD

Devon Live

◆

October 2020

CYCLIST CLIMBS PHYSICAL AND MENTAL MOUNTAINS AFTER HORRIFIC CRASH WHICH NEARLY KILLED HIM

InYourArea, reporting on my successful ascent
of Mount Kilimanjaro

HIT-AND-RUN DRINK DRIVER FACES JAIL FOR SERIOUSLY INJURING CYCLIST ON END TO END RIDE

Road.cc

◆

November 2020

DRINK-DRIVER JAILED FOR LAND'S END CYCLIST HIT-AND-RUN

BBC

JAIL FOR DRINK DRIVER WHO LEFT CYCLIST WITH SERIOUS INJURIES

North Devon Gazette

CYCLIST FORGIVES UNINSURED DRUNK DRIVER
WHO PUT HIM IN INTENSIVE CARE

Cycling Weekly

JEAN-PIERRE DE VILLIERS HAS FORGIVEN
THE DRINK DRIVER WHO NEARLY KILLED HIM

Coventry Telegraph

◆

There are so many questions. I have thought about why it happened. I have no memory of the collision but as well as my injuries to remind me, I still wake up at night with the *smell* of intensive care in my head.

I have been asked what I *feel* about the driver. I feel nothing other than not wanting him to be on the road. I have zero animosity or negativity towards him.

I forgave him straight away. I even feel sorry for him. For me, this was a life-changing experience, but I am grateful to be alive.

'Mr Evans, I want you to know I truly believe that everything happens for a reason. There are consequences and repercussions for what you did to me.

'I really hope that whatever happens to you, you can use the time to heal whatever you need to heal and that you come out of this a better and stronger man.

I forgive you.'

Extract from my court statement

About Jean-Pierre De Villiers

Jean-Pierre De Villiers is a Mental-Performance and Spiritual-Fitness Coach, Inspirational Speaker, Best-Selling Author and Plant-based Athlete.

JP, as he is known, coaches people how to tap into their full potential, thrive under pressure and perform at their best by optimising their energy, transforming their body and mind and spirit. He delivers high impact coaching giving people optimum certainty, energy and obsession, so that they become the CEO of their life.

With almost two decades of experience in high performance and personal coaching, JP is renowned for running transformational events, seminars and challenges globally, stretching people to be their absolute best.

He has worked with thousands of influential men and women who demand the best from themselves and is the author of 9 books. His latest best-selling book 'Self Confidence', teaching psychological skills for self confidence and high performance, is available on Amazon.

Olympic medalists, business leaders, entrepreneurs,

actors and award-winning film directors and producers have benefited from JP's expertise and have relied on him to help them perform at the highest level. JP teaches leading-edge strategies to keep his clients ahead of the game.

As well as speaking internationally, being featured on TedX, and being hired by large global organisations for his high impact coaching skills, Jean-Pierre regularly contributes to publications and features in the media. JP is a professional martial artist, has completed multiple ultra-marathons and other endurance events, is an Ironman triathlete and was voted as health coach of the year. In 2022 JP Ordained as a Buddhist Monk (To further his knowledge of Self-Mastery)

JP was selected as one of the most inspiring people in London, supported by the London Mayor's Office, and has had the honour of speaking in front of the UAE Royal Family.

JP has spoken internationally for Success Resources and Najahi Events, two of the largest seminar promoters in the world, and has shared the stage with some of the world's best speakers (including Les Brown, Dr John Demartini, Lisa Nichols, Jay Abraham, Robert Kiyosaki, Jay Shetty and many more) and has represented the No.1 High Performance Coach in the world, Tony Robbins, throughout Europe, South Africa, the UK and The Middle East.

'I am a high impact speaker, mindset and spiritual-fitness coach, working in the energy management and optimisation game. My expertise lies in optimising your certainty, energy and obsession in your life.

My passion is creating powerful leaders. And my coaching is bespoke and based on what works at the highest end of the market, having worked with the best of the best.'

JP is one of the leading coaches in the world, he has the ability to not only show us linear strategic moves, but also ways to make life better, stronger, and more exciting.

Lisa Nichols

JP is a brilliant man.

Jay Abraham *The 9.4 Billion Dollar Man*

JP regularly takes CEOs, athletes and celebrities out of their comfort zones and into better, more meaningful lives. These high-achieving people aren't easy to work with.

Daniel Priestley

Contact

Website: *www.jeanpierredevilliers.com*

Email: *jpdv@jeanpierredevilliers.com*

Join JP's LIV100 Mastermind Coaching:

https://www.jpdvperformance.com/liv100

Printed in Great Britain
by Amazon

14202410R00066